ACTION!

Contents

D1329280

Jan Burchett
and Sara Vogler

Story illustrated by
Martin Chatterton

Heinemann

Before Reading

Find out about

- How films make people look as if they are doing daring things

Tricky words

- dangerous
- building
- cushion
- crocodiles
- impossible
- special effects
- instead
- appearance

Introduce these tricky words and help the reader when they come across them later!

Text starter

When you watch a film, it looks as if the film star is doing dangerous things. Really, it is a stunt man or woman. Sometimes the stunts are impossible for people to do, so special effects are used instead.

Behind the Scenes

When you watch a film it looks
as if the film star is doing
dangerous things.
But it is not the film star.
It is a stunt man or stunt woman.

But are these things really
so dangerous?
Here are some stunt men
jumping off a building.

It looks very dangerous!
But you do not see the big cushion
that the men will land on.

Have you seen James Bond do dangerous things?
He has to escape from crocodiles, ski over cliffs and jump from burning cars.

Gary Powell has done stunts for three James Bond films. He is said to be one of the best stunt men ever.

Gary Powell has also done stunts for *Harry Potter* films.

Some film stars like to do their own stunts.

Jackie Chan has done more stunts than any other film star.

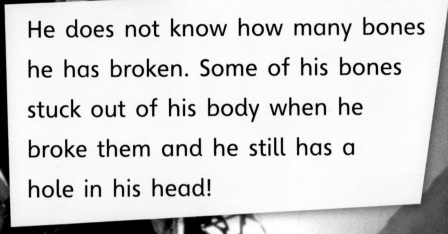

He does not know how many bones he has broken. Some of his bones stuck out of his body when he broke them and he still has a hole in his head!

Sometimes the stunts are impossible for people to do. Special effects are used instead. The people who make special effects use computers.

In the Spiderman films, Spiderman did not swing from building to building.

But the computer made it look as if he did!

Some people who work on films change the appearance of the actors. In the *Lord of the Rings* films 16,000 ears and feet were made for the actors who played the hobbits.

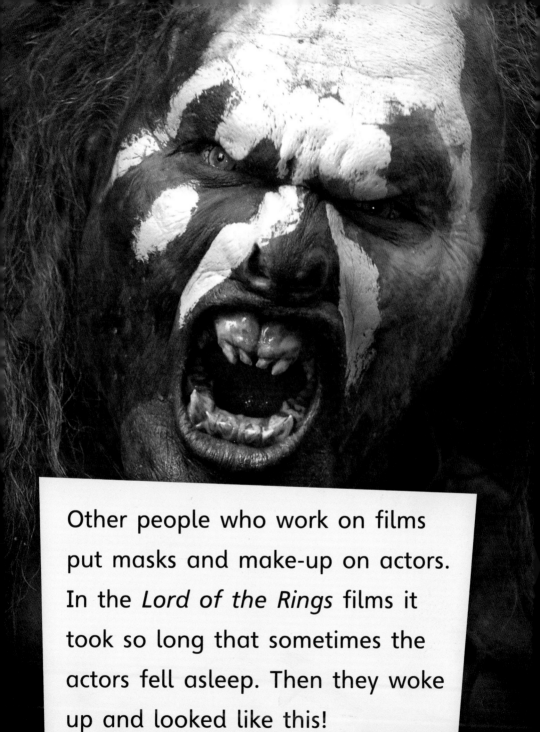

Other people who work on films put masks and make-up on actors. In the *Lord of the Rings* films it took so long that sometimes the actors fell asleep. Then they woke up and looked like this!

Would you like to be a stunt man?
Would you like to make the masks
or do the make-up?
Or would you like to be the star?

Quiz

Text Detective

- How do film makers make special effects if stunts are impossible to do?
- Do you think film stars should do their own stunts?

Word Detective

- Phonic Focus: Long vowel phonemes
  Page 9: Sound out the four phonemes in 'bones'.
  What long vowel phoneme can you hear?
- Page 6: Find a word meaning 'risky'.
- Page 6: Find three verbs describing the dangerous things James Bond does.

Super Speller

Read these words:

really   work   own

Now try to spell them!

HA! HA! HA!

 Q Who is the best underwater spy?

A James Pond!

In this story

 Sami Search

 Jim

 The police officer

Tricky words

- robbery
- jewellers
- investigate
- mobile
- police
- building
- aliens
- mystery

Introduce these tricky words and help the reader when they come across them later!

Story starter

Sami Search wants to be a detective when he grows up. He thinks he is great at solving crimes, but he always gets things wrong. When he hears of a robbery at the jewellers, Sami Search investigates. Let him tell you about his latest case.

The Case of the Jewel Robber

I was in the corner shop when I heard there had been a robbery. Someone had robbed the jewellers.

I had to investigate.

"This is a case for me," I said.

I got out my notebook.

I went down the High Street.
I saw a man with a big bag.

He was talking on his mobile phone.
"Hello, it's Jim," he said. "I've got
the jewels."
Then I knew who he was.
Jim was the jewel robber!

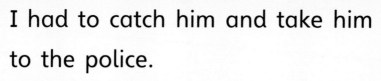

I had to catch him and take him to the police.

But first I followed him. He might be going to rob another shop!

Jim went round the corner.

Where was he going?

He went inside a big building.

I went in after him.

There were aliens and a
spaceship in a room.
"That's odd!" I thought.
But I couldn't stop.
I had to follow Jim.

What kind of building
has Sami walked into?

Jim went round another corner.

I saw Spiderman climbing a wall.

"That's odd!" I thought.

But I couldn't stop.

I had to follow Jim.

Jim went outside to some caravans.

They had stars on their doors.

Now I knew what he was going

to do.

He was going to rob the caravans!

I had to stop him. I jumped on him and we fell to the ground. His bag burst open and jewels went everywhere.

"Call the police!" I shouted.

Just then another man burst out
of one of the caravans.

He had a bag in his hand.

He must have come to help me,
but he fell over us!

His bag burst open and jewels
went everywhere.
A police officer came running up.

"Here is the robber," I said,
pointing at Jim. "And here are
the stolen jewels."
"They are not real jewels,"
said Jim. "They are for a film!"

"**These** are real jewels and **this** is the real robber," said the police officer as she arrested the man who had fallen over us. "He was robbing the film stars' caravans."

"Of course!" I said.

I got out my notebook.

"Another mystery solved," I said.

"Case closed!"

Quiz

Text Detective

- What were the clues that made Sami think Jim was the jewel robber?
- Did Sami help the police catch the real robber?

Word Detective

- Phonic Focus: Long vowel phonemes
  Page 24: Sound out the four phonemes in 'round'.
  What long vowel phoneme can you hear?
- Page 18: Find a word that means 'find out about'.
- Page 25: Find a word made up of two shorter words.

Super Speller

Read these words:

talking   couldn't   over

Now try to spell them!

HA! HA! HA!

Q What's the difference between a jeweller and a jailer?

A One sells watches and the other watches cells.